You Have the Power

Working Hard

I0901369

Seth Matthas

SOCIAL AND EMOTIONAL LEARNING FOR THE REAL WORLD™

Rosen Classroom™

You can do anything.
You have to work hard!

What do you want?
Think about it.

Do you want to play soccer?

Play every day.
Learn to score a goal!

Do you want to play piano?

Practice every day.
Try new songs!

Do you want to learn to skate?

Skate every day.
Get up each time you fall.

You have the power.
You can do well!